In the Shadow
of His Wings

In the Shadow of His Wings

PSALMS OF PEACE IN TIMES OF TROUBLE

ALICE PONGRACZ

WESTBOW
PRESS®
A DIVISION OF THOMAS NELSON
& ZONDERVAN

Scriptures taken from the Holy Bible, New International Version®, NIV®. Copyright © 1973, 1978, 1984, 2011 by Biblica, Inc.™ Used by permission of Zondervan. All rights reserved worldwide. www.zondervan.com The "NIV" and "New International Version" are trademarks registered in the United States Patent and Trademark Office

This book is a work of non-fiction. Unless otherwise noted, the author and the publisher make no explicit guarantees as to the accuracy of the information contained in this book and in some cases, names of people and places have been altered to protect their privacy.

WestBow Press books may be ordered through booksellers or by contacting:

WestBow Press
A Division of Thomas Nelson & Zondervan
1663 Liberty Drive
Bloomington, IN 47403
www.westbowpress.com
1 (866) 928-1240

Because of the dynamic nature of the Internet, any web addresses or links contained in this book may have changed since publication and may no longer be valid. The views expressed in this work are solely those of the author and do not necessarily reflect the views of the publisher, and the publisher hereby disclaims any responsibility for them.

Any people depicted in stock imagery provided by Thinkstock are models, and such images are being used for illustrative purposes only. Certain stock imagery © Thinkstock.

ISBN: 978-1-9736-1890-4 (sc)
ISBN: 978-1-9736-1889-8 (hc)
ISBN: 978-1-9736-1891-1 (e)

Library of Congress Control Number: 2018901870

Print information available on the last page.

WestBow Press rev. date: 03/22/2018

Table of Contents

After The Storm

*I*ntroduction

In The Shadow of His Wings is a 30 day devotional based on the book of Psalms. As each of us go through times of troubles, or what we may see as storms in our life, these are the times that we need to draw nearer to God. In this devotional, God's Word teaches how to look at these troubled times, how to identify the truth in a world of lies, and how to understand God's faithful love. He is our refuge, our stronghold, and everything we need.

My prayer for you is that you will find God's Word as a comfort and guide as you weather the storms. Know that the storms will come. I pray that you are grounded in God's Word, so you find confidence that you are standing on the Rock and will not be shaken.

Even in the tough times, we all need to know that there is joy because our salvation is through Jesus' gift of love. Our joy is not based on our circumstances, but on the love we accept from God.

Know His love

 Know His comfort

  Know He is faithful

   Know that He is our mighty warrior

   Know who is fighting our battles for us

I've given you my prayer. There's a place for you to take the time to write out your prayers to God. Tell Him what is really on your heart. Give Him your praise for what He has done for you.

On My Own

Vulnerable

You Are Not Alone or Helpless

> I love you, LORD, my strength. The LORD is my rock, my fortress and my deliverer; my God is my rock, in whom I take refuge, my shield and the horn of my salvation, my stronghold. (Psalm 18:1-2)

My God is...name it as David did. I praise God for all He has been for me and for all He has done for me. I praise God for seeing me through the battles—the times I've been oh so vulnerable and helpless.

As Psalm 18 continues, I see David's prayer as my prayer. In times of need, I call to the Lord "and I have been saved" (v. 3b). He saved me when I was most vulnerable "from my enemies" (v. 3b), from "the cords of death" (v. 4a), and He saved me when "destruction overwhelmed me" (v. 4b). Even as I see the risks of attack all around me, and as I see my vulnerability of having the worst outcome possible in my mind, I can call out to God. I am not alone. This feeling of helplessness and of being overwhelmed comes when I look to myself for a way out or a solution.

Instead I can call upon my Lord. "In my distress, I called to the LORD; I called to my God for help. From His temple He heard my voice; my cry came before Him, into His ears" (v. 6). He hears me! When I cry out to God and tell Him all that is in my heart, He hears me! I can bring to Him anything and everything, and He hears me even when it's just a whisper or

1

whimper. As a parent is so attuned to his or her newborn baby, the faintest cry is heard. Call out! I need you, God.

He hears my cry and comes to me. "He reached down from on high and took hold of me; He drew me out of deep waters. He rescued me from my powerful enemy, from my foes, who were too strong for me" (v. 16–17). No matter my situation, no matter how vulnerable I feel, and no matter if I believe there is no hope, He is my God, the one in whom I can put my trust. He will come!

Even in my vulnerability, I turn to God and keep His Word close to my heart. "He rescued me because He delighted in me" (v. 19b). He knows my heart. Even in my temporary doubts and fears, He knows my heart.

As I turn my face away from my enemies who surround me and turn it to God, I am no longer vulnerable. I can do anything with Him by my side. "With your help I can advance against a troop, with my God I can scale a wall" (v. 29). He takes my weakness and gives me confidence.

"As for God, His way is perfect" (v. 30a). I may ask, why? Why am I in this situation? Why me? Why is this so difficult? I need again to take my eyes off me and trust His way. "For who is God besides the LORD? And who is the Rock except our God?" (v. 31). I can trust in my God, my Rock, and let Him have His perfect way in my life.

And praise Him! "The LORD lives! Praise be to my Rock! Exalted be God my Savior!" (v. 46). I find I keep my eyes on God, as I praise Him for all He has done, is doing, and will do in my life. "Therefore I will praise you, LORD, among the nations; I will sing the praises of your name" (v. 49).

David started the psalm praising God as his rock, fortress, deliverer, refuge, shield, salvation, and stronghold. He knows his God, his Lord. He knows God is always with him. And his heart sings praises. No longer vulnerable, he is in God's care. I have so much to gain with this way of life—a life of focus on my God in every situation, and a life of praise for all He has done for me.

My Prayer

My Lord, my Rock, my salvation. You are worthy of my praises. I give you my fears and my worries. I trust in your perfect ways. You are my God, who hears my cries and comes.

_____
_____
_____
_____
_____
_____
_____
_____
_____
_____
_____
_____
_____
_____
_____
_____
_____
_____
_____
_____
_____
_____
_____
_____
_____
_____
_____

Wait In Hope

Lay Your Fears in God's Hands

A text. A newscast. A telephone call. All telling of the imminent danger looming over so many towns downstream from the dam. People anxiously waiting, listening, wondering, and praying. *Is it now? Should we go or should we stay?* Then the message goes out to take shelter. Evacuate to a safe place. Take with you only the essentials.

But where should we go? Can I get there safely or soon enough? Scenes of cars stuck in traffic still in the path of the danger. Families separated. Families not knowing if those in danger made it to safety.

A real-life scenario was still unfolding as I wrote this. Not a movie I've seen in so many versions. Superman was not going to fly in to place the boulder to stop the water. Instead, I saw the hard work of crews scrambling to fix the problem in time. While townspeople and families anxiously await and wonder— whether they should stay or go. Be it flooding, hurricanes, storms, or tornadoes, they prepare and then they wait.

Or is the danger more personal? Am I experiencing the imminent danger of a loved one's failing health, waiting for the test results to come in? Or has a friend been told that she cannot have children? Maybe I'm just wondering whether my children are safe.

It can be so difficult to wait. I have a need to know what's coming so that I can prepare. I can wait in fear and feel helpless. Or I can wait in hope. Or maybe a little of both. Which one is dominating my thoughts right now? Fear and worry have a way of taking over my mind and overshadowing any hope.

> We wait in hope for the LORD; He is our help and our shield. (Psalm 33:20)

I lay my fears and worries into God's capable hands. I lift up my prayers to God and let go. He knows what I am going through, and He knows the outcome that lies ahead for me. I trust in Him.

> He says, 'Be still and know that I am God'. (Psalm 46:10a)

> 'For I know the plans I have for you' says the LORD, 'plans to prosper you and not to harm you, to give you hope and a future.' (Jeremiah 29:11)

My Prayer

Lord God, I give you my worries and my fears. You are my God, and I need to learn to be better about trusting in you. My today and my future are in your hands. Help me to wait in hope.

_____

_____

_____

_____

_____

_____

_____

_____

_____

_____

_____

_____

_____

_____

_____

_____

_____

_____

_____

_____

_____

_____

_____

_____

_____

Casting My Cares

Let Go and Let God

I'm a problem-solver. I've been a mom for thirty years. A manager for twenty years. Youth leader for several years. Homeowner, friend, daughter, wife—whatever role I'm in, I'm a problem-solver. Even if I'm in a group and someone comes up to us with a question, I seem to be the one they look to for the answer. My face must say, "Can I help you?"

As a manager, I've been taught active listening skills, troubleshooting, problem-solving techniques, negotiating skills, and team building. Ultimately, the burden lies on my shoulders. It's a "me" environment—what can I do, what advice can I give, and what support is needed to achieve the best outcome?

So how do I let go and let God care for me? It's so easy for me to continue in this role of problem-solver in my own life.

> Cast your cares on the LORD and He will sustain
> you; He will never let the righteous be shaken.
> (Psalm 55:22)

The word *"cast"* is such a visually accurate term for what I need to do. The fishermen would cast their net or their line away from them. There's a well calculated destination to be reached. They don't just cast hither and yon, hoping to get one. Where do I want to cast my cares? Away from me and into the loving arms of my God. I shouldn't go to everyone else to find my answers, nor keep it all to myself.

If I keep the problem-solving all to myself, I'm being very prideful. In order to give my cares into His hands, I have to let go.

> Humble yourselves, therefore, under God's mighty hand, that He may lift you up in due time. Cast all your anxiety on Him because He cares for you. (1 Peter 5:6–7)

> Praise be to the Lord, to God our Savior, who daily bears our burdens. (Psalm 68:19)

He will sustain me. I have no doubt I can find my own solution. But am I choosing the best one for me? I know if I put my trust in Him, He will lead me, care for me, and sustain me. Jesus teaches me so well to come to Him and to let go.

> Come to me, all you who are weary and burdened, and I will give you rest. Take my yoke upon you and learn from me, for I am gentle and humble in heart, and you will find rest for your souls. For my yoke is easy and my burden is light. (Matthew 11:28–30)

If I hang on to my worries, burdens, fears, and cares, I am on sinking sand. Tossed by the waves. Unsure of what to do. Yet if I turn to God and stand on His promises, I am on solid ground. Through prayer and study of His Holy Word, I will build that solid foundation. As I talk to Him, I receive His wise counsel. In His Word, I see His promises and know where to put my trust. He will never let me be moved.

> Therefore everyone who hears these words of mine and puts them into practice is like a wise man who built his house on the rock. The rain

came down, the streams rose, and the winds blew and beat against that house; yet it did not fall, because it had its foundation on the rock. (Matthew 7:24–25)

Oh, how comforting to know my house is built on the Rock. I have Jesus as my foundation, and I will not be moved. The storm may come, but I can cast my cares on the Lord and He will sustain me.

My Prayer

Lord, I claim these promises you have given me. I thank you
that I can place my trust in you. Because you love me, you take
my burdens and care for me.

_____

_____

_____

_____

_____

_____

_____

_____

_____

_____

_____

_____

_____

_____

_____

_____

_____

_____

_____

_____

_____

_____

_____

_____

_____

_____

_____

_____

Times Of Trouble

Do Not Lose Heart

A message received, "Just letting you know we're ok." There had been another attack in London recently. Our family was visiting England. Not close to the place of attack but too close from our perspective. So many thoughts and emotions—fear, relief, anger, and worry. Our response was to pray for protection.

I hear so often we are in times of trouble. This world has gone crazy. Our faith, everyone's faith, is under attack. As Christians, more and more believers are experiencing their faith being oppressed. The battle is coming closer and closer to each of us personally.

Recently I had to take a stand at work on a subject I was asked to help facilitate a discussion for. My response, I'm sorry but you are asking me to deny my God. I can't participate. I knew I had to draw the line. The challenge to my faith just came a lot closer than ever before.

So why was I surprised that my faith was being attacked? Since the beginning of man, Satan has been the enemy of those who love and follow God. The battle has been waged again and again—Israel in captivity for 400 years, Daniel in the fiery furnace, Saul persecuting Christians, and then Paul along with the church being persecuted by the Jews and Romans. So I ask myself again, why am I surprised that believers are being oppressed and we are living in times of trouble? God is not surprised.

God knows what it means for me to be a believer amongst non-believers. He knows the aggression I may experience, and He is my safe place and my strength through it all.

> The LORD is a refuge for the oppressed, a stronghold in times of trouble. (Psalm 9:9)

No matter what I am experiencing or fearing, I am not alone, and through God's power (not mine) I will come through victorious.

> But we have this treasure in jars of clay to show that this all surpassing power is from God and not from us. (2 Corinthians 4:7)

I can face the trials in my life in confidence. "We are hard pressed on every side, but not crushed; perplexed, but not in despair; persecuted, but not abandoned; struck down, but not destroyed" (2 Corinthians 4:8–9). I can claim these truths because He is my refuge and my stronghold. He has already won each of these battles that I have to go through.

And in that, I have hope.

> Therefore we do not lose heart. Though outwardly we are wasting away, yet inwardly we are being renewed day by day. For our light and momentary troubles are achieving for us an eternal glory that far outweighs them all. So we fix our eyes not on what is seen, but on what is unseen, since what is seen is temporary, but what is unseen is eternal. (2 Corinthians 4:16–18)

I can stand up and face the challenges to my faith. I do not fight the battles alone. Even though I may be battle weary, I can run into the safe place of refuge—God's love and strength.

> For in the day of trouble He will keep me safe
> in His dwelling; He will hide me in the shelter
> of His sacred tent and set me high upon a rock.
> (Psalm 27:5)

My Prayer

God, I don't know what battles or troubles are ahead for me. I claim your strength and your power on my journey. I will not be defeated. I can stand up and face this world, because I stand with you. The victory is yours. The message received from you—"Just letting you know you'll be ok."

Because He Said So

Keep Me in Perfect Peace

The foundation of my faith in God is claiming and believing in His Word, the Holy Bible. His Word is truth.

> For the word of the LORD is right and true; He is faithful in all He does. (Psalm 33:4)

When I know God's Word to be true, and truly believe it, I can find peace in my life. Why? Because He said so.

In my first apartment, I would wake up in fear from time to time, not knowing what woke me up. I would start to pray for God to keep me safe. What came to mind was the Israelites being kept safe from the last plague by putting the blood of the sacrificial lamb above their door. Obviously, my landlord would not appreciate if I actually did that in the middle of the night. But I had something better—prayer. So I would pray the blood of Jesus over each and every opening to my home and claim the protection of God. By the time I was done, I was at peace, and I could fall asleep.

Every home I've lived in I've asked for God's protection and blessing. And from time to time, I've felt the need to pray the blood of Jesus to keep me safe.

In my current home, I watched it being built from the ground up. God had called me to this home and neighborhood. Only He knew why. I gave Him this home, and the foundation is covered in God's Word. Family and friends helped me to write scriptures all over the concrete, and then we prayed for His blessing of my home—His home.

"In peace I will lie down and sleep, for you alone, LORD, make me dwell in safety" (Psalm 4:8) is one of the scriptures in my bedroom. What a beautiful prayer to say each night as I go to sleep.

Because He said so, I can trust He is going to watch over me, and I can rest in Him. Not just to sleep but to be at peace. I can let go of any and all of my fears, worries, and troubles in my life—all of them.

> You will keep in perfect peace those whose minds are steadfast, because they trust in you. (Isaiah 26:3)

I cannot find peace on my own. Peace is a gift that comes from God alone. For me, no matter how hard I try to work things out or let it go, I keep bringing it back to try to "fix it". No wonder there are times I can't find peace. I need to claim His peace.

> The LORD turn His face toward you and give you peace. (Numbers 6:26)

> Peace I leave with you; my peace I give you. (John 14:27a)

Because He said so! What am I waiting for! I can take His gift of peace.

I look for peace in my life as I walk through the day. Am I in chaos, stressed, or worried? God is peace. So why am I experiencing everything but peace? "For God is not a God of disorder but peace" (1 Corinthians 14:33a). If I find myself not in peace about decisions before me, I turn my eyes to God and ask for His wisdom. If I don't know His peace, then I won't move forward. I will wait for His will and His peace.

You see, this peace is so much more than I can ever fully understand. How do I find peace when finances are low? How do I have peace when my future is uncertain? How do I live in peace, no matter what the circumstances are? I keep my eyes on God, my Lord. I can't keep my eyes on the world that wants to tell me all is lost and there is no hope. If this is what I'm living in, then it's time to walk away and return to God.

> And the peace of God, which transcends all understanding, will guard your hearts and your minds in Christ Jesus. (Philippians 4:7)

Because He said so, I can have this peace.

There is always hope in God. As His child, I know God, my Father, has my future in His hands. The world is not in control of my life, unless I let it. My hope lies in God, and with that hope, I can have peace.

> May the God of hope fill you with all joy and peace as you trust in Him, so that you may overflow with hope by the power of the Holy Spirit." (Romans 15:13)

When I claim His Word, His truth, then I will know peace. Because He said so, I can have this peace.

> Now may the Lord of peace Himself give you peace at all times and in every way. The Lord be with all of you. (2 Thessalonians 3:16)

My Prayer

Lord God, I give you my today, my future, and my life. I trust in you for what lies ahead, and I know that you hold me in your precious hands. I can have peace through you and you alone. Thank you for the joy, hope, and peace that are in you. I know this to be true, because you said so.

_____

_____

_____

_____

_____

_____

_____

_____

_____

_____

_____

_____

_____

_____

_____

_____

_____

_____

_____

_____

_____

_____

_____

_____

Running on Empty

God's Bottomless Well of Love

It was a beautiful day on the Santorini Island. Crystal blue waters surrounding us, the breezes keeping us cool, and shopping keeping us entertained. The day started with a gondola ride up to the top of the island. I watched other tourists brave the donkey ride up and down the winding road. I was envious of the adventure they were having. Come the end of the day and seeing the long lines to take the gondola back down to our shore boat, I had the idea to just walk it—all the way down the island. So a friend, my daughter and I started the trek. I was thrilled to be able to make this part of our trip, until I realized what this road held for us. I learned quickly how slippery the marble path was and the challenge of missing the plops of donkey dung. Add to that, the incline was much steeper than I anticipated. Less than 5 minutes into this walk, my thighs were shaking. I've never been much of an athlete. What should I do? Looking back up the hill wasn't promising, so I chose the downhill path of donkey littered switch backs. My friend, an athlete, left us in the dust. My daughter slowed her pace and cheered on her mom—every step of the way. I never saw the view, but remained focused on each step making it to the smaller goal of each turn. Ready for the next level. I prayed at every step to find something deep within me to keep going. Motivation of not missing the shore boat in the forefront kept me from not giving up. If I could have figured out how to hijack a donkey walking by, I would have jumped on one. Somehow I made it with just minutes to spare. Later that evening, reclined in my bed in our cabin, I asked for one thing—a lily to lie on my chest for I knew soon I was probably going to "die" or so it seemed.

What an experience! I've never had to pull from so deep to try and find something to keep me going. It was so much more than all the times I prayed for my car to just make it to a gas station before running out of gas. I once thought the nights of staying up consoling a sick baby, and finding the energy to make it through the next day at work were tough. Somehow I made it through these experiences when I didn't think I could. I know without a doubt, God came along side me to sustain me.

> Surely God is my help; the LORD is the one who sustains me. (Psalm 54:4)

But what if my faith is on empty? What if love inside me has gone dry? The joy is gone. Those have been the most difficult paths to walk down. Each day was like my Santorini walk— one step in front of the other and finding my way back to God.

Paul's prayer for the church in Ephesus became my prayer: a prayer for God to strengthen me with power through the Holy Spirit, not on my strength; a prayer to ask Christ to dwell in and fill my heart; a prayer to learn how to be deeply rooted in His love, with no more doubts; and a prayer to be filled to the fullness of God.

In other words, when empty, I need to call on my Savior.

> I pray that out of His glorious riches He may strengthen you with power through His Spirit in your inner being, so that Christ may dwell in your hearts through faith. And I pray that you, being rooted and established in love, may have power, together with all the Lord's holy people, to grasp how wide and long and high and deep is the love of Christ, and to know this love that surpasses knowledge—that you may be filled to

21

the measure of all the fullness of God. (Ephesians 3:16–19)

There is no empty with God as the center of my life, my resource. I have found how deep I can go to find the strength to make it through anything. It's the never-ending bottomless well of God's love.

My Prayer

Thank you, Lord that you are always there to sustain me. I will never be empty when I am filled with your love.

_____
_____
_____
_____
_____
_____
_____
_____
_____
_____
_____
_____
_____
_____
_____
_____
_____
_____
_____
_____
_____
_____
_____
_____
_____
_____
_____
_____

The Journey

Road Trip Tips

Road Trip! What comes to mind when I hear that? Excitement, bad memories, adventures, or long hot days squished in the car with your siblings and no air-conditioning?

Each road trip I've been on has been a lesson on what to do and what not to do. What should I bring? Do I know the road ahead? Am I prepared? Am I with the right people? Do I love the thrill of being spontaneous? Can I handle changes in the plan?

You see the road trip is not about the destination but the journey to the destination. If I'm saying, "are we there yet?", then I'm not enjoying the beauty along the way. I may miss the people I could meet and be blessed by. Or I could miss the opportunities that come from being lost, to problem-solve and find my way back on the road.

I've had my share of adventures on my journeys—from flat tires, to running out of gas (twice), to finding myself stuck in mud by taking a wrong road, to being ill prepared for the weather, sick children, bad food, and injuries. Need I go on? These journeys also included connecting with my children in ways that couldn't have happened otherwise. I have memories of laughing so hard at my son's humor that I had to pull off the road, and showing them the thrill of reaching a destination, by traveling a winding road, to find God's love in the beauty of His nature.

On those tough adventures, when I had to put my trust in God, He was always there. I had a car full of kids once, after a long day, and found myself a little further down the highway wondering how I got there. I dozed off. Once I realized what happened, I was so scared and so grateful that God's hands protected us all.

God has been there in every part of my life: In all my comings and goings; each step; every decision; the good, the bad and the ugly. I've never known a time when He wasn't taking care of me.

> The LORD will keep you from all harm—He will watch over your life; the LORD will watch over your coming and going both now and forevermore. (Psalm 121:7–8)

I don't know what the next journey will be for me. I can't assume each road trip is going to be easygoing. I'm not going to get everything I expect along the way. But I do know that my travel partner, God, will always be with me.

Here are some Road Trip (Life) tips:

1. He will take care of my needs: "And my God will meet all your needs according to the riches of His glory in Christ Jesus" (Philippians 4:19).
2. Zero visibility requires putting my faith in God: "For we live by faith, not by sight" (2 Corinthians 5:7).
3. Road weary? I will press on: "Let us not become weary in doing good, for at the proper time we will reap a harvest if we do not give up" (Galatians 6:9).
4. Need Directions? Follow God to the destination He wants me to go: "Direct me in the path of your commands, for there I find delight" (Psalm 119:35).

5. Choose my travel companions wisely: "Therefore encourage one another and build each other up, just as in fact you are doing" (1 Thessalonians 5:11).
6. Detour to stay on the right road: "And we know that in all things God works for the good of those who love Him, who have been called according to His purpose" (Romans 8:28).
7. Have the right equipment: "All Scripture is God-breathed and is useful for teaching, rebuking, correcting and training in righteousness, so that the servant of God may be thoroughly equipped for every good work" (2 Timothy 3:16–17).

As I recall all the journeys I've taken, I've learned one thing above all else. My God is faithful. He will always be on this journey with me. I can trust Him to take the wheel and lead me on the path He has chosen for me. What beautiful peace that brings to me.

> For I have always been mindful of your unfailing love and have lived in reliance on your faithfulness. (Psalm 26:3)

My Prayer

God, let's do this road trip together. Teach me to trust that you have my best in mind, no matter what path we take together. Let me see the joy and beauty along the way. May I find laughter in my wrong turns, and equip me to find the right path. On the road again—with you!

God Is My Word, My Shield

Listen to God's Truth

"Liar, liar, pants on fire" was a common childhood chant. Today we call it out differently as "fake news" found on the news channels or internet. In WWII, lies were the propaganda of the Japanese through leaflet dropping or Tokyo Rose on the radio. The Apostle Paul continually faced crowds stirred up through the lies from people threatened by the truth Paul was preaching about Jesus. From the beginning of time, Satan has used lies to draw God's children away from Him.

God's Word, the Holy Bible, is the one truth I can use to stand up against the lies from the world. When the world comes at me with lies and deceit, I can put my hope in God's Word.

> You are my refuge and my shield; I have put my
> hope in your word. (Psalm 119:114)

God's Word is the shield that protects me as the lies come at me, to pierce me, to destroy me, and to make me doubt my faith. How do I protect myself from the attacks from Satan? I take up my shield as part of the full armor of God.

> In addition to all this, take up the shield of faith,
> with which you can extinguish all the flaming
> arrows of the evil one. (Ephesians 6:16)

As God is my refuge, I draw near to Him and listen to His truth. When I doubt, who am I really listening to? Jesus clearly identifies Satan for who he is. "For he is a liar and the father of lies." (John 8:44c). Then Jesus goes on to promise that "whoever

28

belongs to God hears what God says" (v. 47a). The truth, God's truth, is my shield of faith.

As a believer, I'm so surprised when I find myself caught up and believing the lies. The lies when I believe I'm not loved, not good enough, or a failure. Or I let my past creep in, and I believe I'm not really forgiven. Somehow I let myself listen to the lies. I like the term "stinkin' thinkin'". Those are the thoughts of unbelief that take over my thoughts. Those are lies. They are not from God.

I say "no, I'm a child of God and I'm not going to believe those lies." Then I can go to Him in prayer and claim His promises from His Word. I learn again to walk away from the sources of those lies.

In Psalm 1, the psalmist describes 3 phases of how easily I can get caught up in the wicked schemes of Satan, and can find myself pierced by one of his flaming arrows.

First, I am warned not to "walk in step with the wicked" (v. 1a). Who am I spending casual time with? Or what radio talk show host, music, or interesting "harmless" internet article did I fill my mind with?

Second, nor am I to "stand in the way that sinners take" (v. 1b). If I'm walking, I'm in motion and can keep going. But now I stand and give more time to the lies. I'm listening longer.

Third, I am not to "sit in the company of mockers" (v. 1c). That's when I sit down and become engaged. The more I listen to those mocking God and less time with Him, I believe in their lies.

Psalm 1:1 also says "Blessed is the one who...." does not walk, stand or sit with the wicked. "But whose delight is in the law of the LORD, and who meditates on His law day and night" (v.

2a). The blessing is in being in His presence, and taking refuge in Him. His Word is my shield to protect me from the lies. My hope is in His Word. That's where I put my faith—in my loving and faithful God.

So when the world (Satan) tries to attack me, I can return the lies with the truth. I speak the Word of God out loud, and as often as I need, and am victorious.

My Prayer

Lord, help me to fight the battles of lies with your truth. I delight in the time we have together. I grow strong from being in your Word of truth, and I am prepared to fight this battle with you.

_____

_____

_____

_____

_____

_____

_____

_____

_____

_____

_____

_____

_____

_____

_____

_____

_____

_____

_____

_____

_____

_____

_____

_____

_____

Sing Again

Carry a Smaller Bag

I have a bag. Sometimes my bag is empty and light, and sometimes it's heavy and full. That depends solely on me. You see, it's up to me what I put in my bag and what to leave there—to drag around with me wherever I go. Or it's up to me what I take out of my bag and leave it where it belongs.

What's in my bag? Just about everything! Before I get out of bed, I start filling my bag with all I need to do today and all I need to resolve at work today. Mind you, some (many) are not even mine to resolve. Of course, I also keep track of my family's "to do" lists.

Then there are the worries. They go in the bag, too. They sound something like this…"How can I get _____ done?" "How can I ever afford_____?" Let's not forget all of the "What if____" thoughts.

I can't forget the whispers of my insecurities that jump in my bag from time to time. If I work harder or longer, maybe I'll be good enough. If I do everything right, maybe I will be liked or accepted.

The list can go on and on—grief, not enough time, heartaches, and demands on me.

The bag is life. Yep…no getting out of it. It's not about keeping all of these things away, but about what I am going to do about them.

> Come to me, all you who are weary and
> burdened, and I will give you rest. Take my yoke
> upon you and learn from me, for I am gentle and
> humble in heart, and you will find rest for your
> souls. For my yoke is easy and my burden is
> light. (Matthew 11:28–30)

I have a choice. I can drag around my bag and keep filling it up, as if it's all mine to be responsible for. As it gets heavier and heavier, I get wearier and tired. By the end of the day, I wonder what happened!

What happened to my joy? Where's my laughter? The song in my heart is missing.

> Because you are my help, I sing in the shadow of
> your wings. (Psalm 63:7)

You see, I want to come under His wings for refuge and shelter when troubles or difficulties come. But I want to bring my bag, too!

I can't have it both ways. Jesus calls me to come to Him and let go. Drop the bag! I am called to come into His presence, and listen to Him. When I do that, only then do I see my life (and all that's in it) from His perspective.

My bag becomes lighter when I let Him help me lighten the load. And I can sing again.

I realize the time is now for me to get a smaller bag and only carry around the essentials. The time is now for me to leave behind the trash, the things that are not mine and things that don't need to be carried around week after week. And quit putting things back in that I gave away or let go.

What are the essentials that I should carry around?

1) God's unfailing love and faithfulness. "For I have always been mindful of your unfailing love and have lived in reliance on your faithfulness" (Psalm 26:3).
2) The reminder that God has brought me through the tough times, again and again. "The LORD has done great things for us, and we are filled with joy" (Psalm 126:3).
3) Salvation is my source of joy, not the ups and downs of daily life. "Then my soul will rejoice in the LORD and delight in his salvation" (Psalm 35:9).

I would much rather carry around His promises, than a full bag of trash. I would much rather carry joy in my heart, than worries and stress.

My Prayer

Thank you, Lord that I can come into your presence and lay my burdens there. In you, I find my joy. In you, I can sing again. Help me daily to walk close to you and carry a smaller bag!

In My Weakness

God is My Strength

No one wants to admit to their weaknesses. I know I don't. And yet my weaknesses face me every morning as I look in the mirror, and every time I try to do something but can't. This may be my health, my skills, my finances, my habits, or even my spiritual life.

My physical strength has never been my best quality. So when I lived as a single woman and homeowner, I had my challenges. I love to garden and am very capable of maintaining a healthy lawn. But me and my edger…that's another story. One dusky summer evening, I met my limit. The line on the edger was gone. All I had to do was twist off the cap and replace the line. No problem. I've done it before. But tonight it wasn't budging. My hands tried as they might. I looked up and down the street hoping a neighbor was available. No such luck. I tried again from a different angle. The growl escaped from my throat. Really!! Again and again I tried. No luck. At this point, frustration was at my highest and with darkness approaching, my mind was screaming. I hated being a weak woman. This was well beyond my ability. My solution—Wait until tomorrow and buy a new edger.

There will always be something I can't do and others can. Or something I wish I had that I believe others possessed. How easy it is to fall into the well of self-pity. "If only…" I was stronger, smarter, healthier, more confident, or had better habits. Or, "if only…"I hadn't made this mistake or made that decision. I am who I am. I can beat myself up, or I can thank God in my every situation. He is my strength when I am weak.

My flesh and my heart may fail, but God is the strength of my heart and my portion forever. (Psalm 73:26)

Yes, my spirit may falter or my health may fail me. I have a temporary body for my time on earth, until I have it exchanged for a perfect one when I go home to heaven. But I want that healthy body until I do...right? I never want to see my spirit falter either. But as I've experienced, the spiritual battle is real, and I may falter and doubt. Yet, in either case, God has a hold of me and never leaves my side.

Yet I am always with you; you hold me by my right hand. (Psalm 73:23)

What a comfort to know that no matter what I am given to experience—those limitations I'm fighting against—I have a God who is everything I need. He's my portion, and He sustains me.

I cry to you, LORD; I say, "you are my refuge, my portion in the land of the living." (Psalm 142:5)

Every day I can choose. I can choose to complain and become embittered. Or...I can thank my God for the strength I have in Him. I can thank Him for another day. I can praise Him for the opportunity to glorify Him in every situation, even in the midst of my weakness.

You make known to me the path of life; you will fill me with joy in your presence, with eternal pleasures at your right hand. (Psalm 16:11)

My Prayer

Lord, in my weakness, help me to know your strength. I thank you for this life, and this journey I'm on with you. May I find joy in you and glorify you even in my weakness.

_____
_____
_____
_____
_____
_____
_____
_____
_____
_____
_____
_____
_____
_____
_____
_____
_____
_____
_____
_____
_____
_____
_____
_____
_____

Under His Wings

In The Storm

Finding Shelter

I awoke to the sound of the storm bearing down on our little cottage on the cliffs, overlooking the Pacific Ocean. This was no little storm. High winds were buffeting the side of our cottage with nothing to slow the winds down. Doors rattled and rain blew in by drops through the glass door. All night long we listened to the storm raging outside—glad that we were dry and safe inside.

I have been through storms before, nothing as bad as I know others have gone through. But no matter what kind of storm I am in the middle of, I understand and appreciate how vulnerable I am at that moment.

My journey through life is going to encounter personal storms. They are a given. Some are short, but strong and hard. Others may just seem to be never-ending. Some come on suddenly, and I find I am not prepared. Others I see coming, yet I cannot get out of the way.

How I will do in each storm is up to me. Do I find shelter? Do I survive it? Do I find peace and comfort? Do I find the strength to go through it?

Take shelter! Take shelter in the loving arms of God Almighty.

> I long to dwell in your tent forever and take
> refuge in the shelter of your wings. (Psalm 61: 4)

I survived a big "life" storm many years ago, though not on my own. My first inkling in this storm was to just curl up and cry out "why?" I knew I couldn't stay there feeling helpless. A sister in Christ came along side me, and as we studied God's Word, I changed "why?" into "You are my Lord, my God", as Moses frequently cried out to God.

In my storm…I needed to recognize who was my Lord, my God. God, and God alone, was going to get me through the storm. I found this to be such a simple, yet powerful prayer, "You are my Lord, my God".

In my storm…I needed to hold on to His love. "How priceless is your unfailing love, O God! People take refuge in the shadow of your wings" (Psalm 36:7). To know His unfailing love brought healing, peace, and comfort.

In my storm…I knew I didn't want to become resentful, bitter, or "ugly". I am (I was) His child. I know my life has one purpose, which is to glorify Him through my actions and my words. "So whether you eat or drink or whatever you do, do it all for the glory of God" (1 Corinthians 10:31). Wow! That's really tough to do on my own…right? But you see I was not on my own. I had my God right beside me through every moment of my storm. I knew His hands guided me, His words taught me how to live in my storm, and His arms brought me comfort. Only then could my life glorify Him.

In my storm…I drew closer to God. How are you doing in your storm?

My Prayer

Father God, thank you for the storms in my life that they may draw me closer to you. Remind me of your unfailing love, and show me how to glorify you in all things.

_____
_____
_____
_____
_____
_____
_____
_____
_____
_____
_____
_____
_____
_____
_____
_____
_____
_____
_____
_____
_____
_____
_____
_____

Open Arms

All is Well in His Arms

As a young girl, one of my favorite places was sitting in a chair next to my mom—her arm around me, my head on her chest, and listening to the vibration of her voice. All was well.

There's something about coming into her open arms. Knowing I will find comfort, love and hope that all will be well.

I have found that as a mom, I want to give my children the same place to come to. Sometimes all I have to do is open my arms, nothing said, and they fall into my arms. Maybe we just hug and laugh, or have a good cry. We both know we are not alone, and together we can face anything. What a comfort and peace that brings.

I know my God and Father wants to give to me so much more.

> He will cover you with his feathers, and under
> his wings you will find refuge. (Psalm 91:4a)

His arms are always open to me, waiting for me to come—to share my heart's desires, my burdens, or just sit next to Him and listen.

Today is one of those days. It's a cloudy day. I'm snuggled under my fleece blanket and God's Word (and dog) in my lap. All is going to be well.

> For great is his love toward us, and the faithfulness
> of the LORD endures forever. (Psalm 117:2)

My Prayer

Lord, thank you that I can fall into your open arms, and know your love surrounds me like a cozy blanket. In you, I put my trust, and find peace and comfort. I find refuge in you.

Coming Home

Building My Stronghold

So close. Following a familiar path. Knowing soon I'll find rest, shelter and safety. I'm so close to home—my stronghold.

That's how I pictured the scene that happened hundreds of years before at Dover Castle. We drove along the road from the White Cliffs of Dover, along the countryside, and then we turned the corner. There it was! Dover Castle was off in the distance—a stronghold, a place to find rest, and a place to be safe.

Where is my stronghold?

Sometimes I find coming home is my stronghold. I can shut out the world and the day. I find coming home to my family is a place of joy.

But a stronghold is so much more. The definition is "a place that has been fortified so as to protect against attack." I may have a dog at home, but he's not going to protect me from attack.

The question is better asked, WHO is my stronghold?

> He is my loving God and my fortress, my
> stronghold and my deliverer, my shield, in whom
> I take refuge, who subdues peoples under me.
> (Psalm 144:2)

God is who I belong to as His child. I'm His and He will care for me. He will keep me safe and let me heal in His presence.

Any stronghold I try to build all on my own will fail, but in Him I will find a stronghold to last.

How do I build my stronghold in Him?

<u>Prepare</u>: Build it solid. Build it strong. Take my time. The stronghold at Dover had walls easily 15 feet thick. For me, this is done by building a solid foundation on God and trusting in Him.

> Unless the LORD builds the house, the builders labor in vain. (Psalm 127:1)

> Therefore everyone who hears these words of mine and puts them into practice is like a wise man who built his house on a rock. (Matthew 7:24)

<u>Store up for the long siege</u>: In a stronghold, a large supply of food was stored up to sustain the needs of the people. Battles may be quick or very lengthy. Am I prepared for either? I need to keep my eyes on God. As He did for the Israelites in the desert, manna was provided each day. He will sustain me with what I need. I store up by trusting in my God to meet my needs.

> Then Jesus declared, "I am the bread of life. Whoever comes to me will never go hungry, and whoever believes in me will never be thirsty." (John 6:35)

<u>Weapons for the attack</u>: In the castle were rooms filled with weapons of all kinds. For me, taking hold of my weapon is to be in His Word daily. I can know the truth by knowing His Word, so I can fight against the lies that attack and try to lead me astray.

> Take the helmet of salvation and the sword of the
> Spirit, which is the word of God. (Ephesians 6:17)

<u>Heal after the attack</u>: The wounded, who came inside the walls, knew they were safe. They could find rest and healing from the battle outside. I can go to God for shelter, and find rest in Him. In His presence through prayer, I will find peace, healing, and a safe place to rest.

> Whoever dwells in the shelter of the Most High
> will rest in the shadow of the Almighty. (Psalm
> 91:1)

<u>I am not alone</u>: In the stronghold, there were others in the fight, and there was the leader, or the King, or the Laird. The people could trust they would be protected. The same is true with my God. He is faithful, and His love is never-ending. He is always there for me, and I can put my trust in Him.

> But as for me, I will trust in you. (Psalm 55:23c)

> For I have always been mindful of your
> unfailing love and have lived in reliance on your
> faithfulness. (Psalm 26:3)

My Prayer

Thank you, Lord that my stronghold is built on you, my Rock. You guide me with your Word, sustain me in your presence, heal my wounds, and make me stronger. I'm coming home, Lord. I'm coming home to you, my stronghold.

My Soul Finds Rest in God

Finding Rest

> Truly my soul finds rest in God; my salvation comes from him. Truly he is my rock and my salvation; he is my fortress, I will never be shaken. (Psalm 62: 1–2)

In one of my journeys, I was transported to another place—magical and beautiful—for a few weeks. All of my daily routine, people and problems were left behind. I was on vacation (or Holiday, as they say) in England and Scotland.

More than a time away, I found my surroundings to be a place of rest in God. My soul found rest—not just physical rest and relaxation. I was able to let go of everything, so my soul could find rest in Him.

As we walked around stone castles on high mountains, high above the valley on a rock, I became fully aware of what a fortress is really like. Or as we explored the underground tunnels in England, where people hid in WWII waiting for someone to save them from the enemy, I found another type of fortress. These images brought to mind that many have been in need of a fortress to be saved from the battle around them.

The battle around us is real—a hundred years ago or today. The enemy may look different, but the battle will come. We all face different battles—physical, financial, grief, loneliness, etc. The list is endless.

No matter what I face or what fills my day, I can find salvation when I turn to my Lord, run to the fortress high on the rock and there find rest for my soul.

As I headed home, I wondered…How can I be transplanted to another place when I'm home in the real world of my daily life? How can I find a fortress when I get home? How do I find rest for my soul in my busy life?

David shows me how in Psalm 62:

1. Take a step to God. He's waiting for me. This is an action for me to take—to take a step to find this level of rest. "Yes, my soul finds rest in God" (v. 5a).
2. Keep my hope in Him. Not in me or others. "My hope comes from him" (v. 5b).
3. Place my trust in Him. "Trust in Him at all times" (v. 8a).
4. Quit holding on to everything. I need to let go, talk to Him and pour it all out. "pour out your heart to Him" (v. 8b).
5. Let go and let God work in my life and the lives around me. The fixing of my problems does not lie solely on my shoulders, if at all. "Power belongs to you, God." (v. 11b).
6. Rest in the arms of the one who loves me unconditionally and endlessly with a love that never fails. "And with you, Lord, is unfailing love" (v. 12a).

M_y P_{rayer}

Lord, teach me to set aside time—short moments or long holidays—to let my soul find rest in you, and to hold on to my salvation in you. Be my fortress on a rock, so when the storms of life come, I will not be shaken. I will find rest in you.

_____
_____
_____
_____
_____
_____
_____
_____
_____
_____
_____
_____
_____
_____
_____
_____
_____
_____
_____
_____
_____
_____
_____
_____
_____

Be My Rock

Nature's Safe Haven

The barking of the sea lions caught our attention long before we could see them. There they were on the rock, not far from the shore. As our eyes were adjusting to their camouflage, we could see several of them sunbathing on the rock. The treasure hunt was still on. Could we find anymore? The splashing in the water was not only waves, but sea lions frolicking with each other. What a delight!! They had found a safe refuge to live in. The Monterey shoreline is habitat to so much ocean life. Sea lions, otters and birds have found refuge on the rock—safe from people, boaters, and the sharks waiting a little further out looking for a meal.

Even as the storms, wind, and waves pummel the rock, the sea lions have a safe place to stay on the shore side of the rock. Nature has provided a safe haven.

> Be my rock of refuge, to which I can always go;
> give the command to save me, for you are my
> rock and my fortress. (Psalm 71:3)

Be my rock, God…when I need a place to rest. Whether I'm still in the battle or after a long struggle, I have a place to go for rest, even if just for a moment. I can take myself out of the waves and climb on top of the rock and rest. I can be still and wait.

> Be still before the LORD and wait patiently for
> Him. (Psalm 37:7a)

Be my rock, God…when I need a safe haven. The world around me is full of dangers—never knowing at which turn I'll be facing a challenge, an enemy, and a risk. I know God is the one stable place I can go to. I can go to my Rock to find safety, and to be out of the dangerous waters to get a clear perspective on what I'm facing. My Rock—a place to remember He has saved me.

> Grace and peace to you from God our Father and the Lord Jesus Christ, who gave Himself for our sins to rescue us from the present evil age, according to the will of our God and Father, to whom be glory forever and ever. Amen. (Galatians 1:3–5)

Be my rock, God...as I celebrate life with you. My Rock—a place I find joy, a place to laugh and play, and a place to rejoice in your love.

> You turn my wailing into dancing; you removed my sackcloth and clothe me with joy, that my heart may sing your praises and not be silent, LORD my God, I will praise you forever. (Psalm 30:11–12)

Be my rock, God...to protect me in the storms. My Rock—a place to seek shelter until the storm has passed. Even though I may not be out of the storm, I find that the storm is easier to face when I'm with you and in your arms.

> Have mercy on me, my God, have mercy on me, for in you I take refuge. I will take refuge in the shadow of your wings until the disaster has passed. (Psalm 57:1)

My Prayer

Lord, you are my Rock. I can find strength, rest, and shelter when I come to you. You will always be my Rock, and I praise you for your unfailing love.

_____

_____

_____

_____

_____

_____

_____

_____

_____

_____

_____

_____

_____

_____

_____

_____

_____

_____

_____

_____

_____

_____

_____

_____

_____

During The Storm

Let's Do It Together

Waiting and waiting until the storm passes. Our second night in Mexico, in our tent camp, was one of the longest nights in my life. As 75 adults and high school students returned from building houses in a village outside of Tijuana, the dreaded rain began. It was spring, and storms were always a big risk.

Some of us were already wet, so we began the task of trenching around our tents to give the rain a place to drain away from our camp. Soon we were drenched to the skin from a torrential downpour. All I could see was my little area that I worked hard to trench. The water was up to my ankles. Soon the camp was covered in trenches. The water was flowing away slower than the rain came in.

When we completed all we could, I found a small overhang to take cover under, and then it hit—the cold and the exhaustion. Trying to decide what to do next as I ate my dinner, I found that my mind was frozen too. My first priority as first aider was to care for the kids, so this was not the time to get into dry clothes. My teeth started chattering, my muscles weakening, and I was shaking all over. From somewhere deep within, I found the strength to finish my work, leaving nothing else to do but get warm and dry. I found an empty van, and snuggled in to my sleeping bag in dry clothes finally. The bench seat was narrow, but I didn't care. I was safe and sheltered. A peace came over me as I drifted off to sleep.

My prayer during that downpour may not have been exactly the same as David's prayer, but it was very close.

> Have mercy on me, my God, have mercy on me,
> for in you I take refuge. I will take refuge in
> the shadow of your wings until the disaster has
> passed. (Psalm 57:1)

Quite the adventure we had that trip. All made it home safe and sound after building homes for very grateful families.

Not all storms in life are so short lived. Some may last months or even years.

I'm referring to the tough, really tough, life experiences that we may have dealt with in some form—Dementia/Alzheimer's, addictions, life-threatening diseases, abusive relationships, death of a loved one, divorce, or loss of a job. These are the subjects no one wants to talk about, and if we're in the midst of experiencing them, we may choose to hide them from everyone else.

David's prayer is even more relative. "God have mercy on me for I take refuge in you." I won't stop at "have mercy on me". I have a God that I can take refuge in during each long day of these storms. He will keep me safe in the shelter of His wings.

> Wait for the LORD; be strong and take heart and
> wait for the LORD. (Psalm 27:14)

In my prayers for those storms to end, I heard from God that He was still with me. He would tell me to be strong in Him and wait.

In the storms to come, I need to listen to His words of love and encouragement.

> May the Lord Jesus Christ himself and God
> our Father, who loved us and by His grace

gave us eternal encouragement and good hope, encourage your hearts and strengthen you in every good deed and word. (2 Thessalonians 2:16–17)

Every day in the storm, I can trust that He is faithful to care for me.

The LORD is trustworthy in all He promises and faithful in all He does. (Psalm 145:13b)

My Prayer

Thank you, God for being by my side each and every day of the storms you have seen me through. Thank you for taking me under your wings and protecting me. I know there are storms ahead, and you will be there for me. The water may get high, and the storm may seem like it will never end, yet I am confident that there are no storms that you cannot calm in your time. If I must go through the storm, let's do it together.

_____

_____

_____

_____

_____

_____

_____

_____

_____

_____

_____

_____

_____

_____

_____

_____

_____

_____

_____

_____

*H*ide In Plain Sight

Seeing the Lord Glorified in My Life

Rescue me from my enemies, LORD, for I hide myself in you. (Psalm 143:9)

One day on the coast, my husband and I watched two workers out working on a beacon that sat on the top of a small rock near the coastline. They had no way off that rock that we could see, surrounded by the ocean. Eventually, the helicopter returned to get them, after making several attempts to line up just right to rescue each of them.

That's what I think of when I hear the words "rescue me". If I'm surrounded by the enemy, I would want God to just rescue me, take me away, and remove me completely from the situation I'm in.

Only that's not always God's plan. You see, my "enemy" can be so many things or people or situations that I am supposed to be experiencing according to His plan.

My job can be challenging and feels so overwhelming…Lord, rescue me.

My aging body has more aches and pains than I want to experience…Lord, rescue me.

My _____ *(fill in the blank)*…Lord, rescue me.

My enemy can take on the form of anything that influences me to take my eyes off of God.

"Rescue me from my enemies" is to be set free from the influences of my enemy on my mind, my attitude, and my life. I can't let the enemy win by letting my response be influenced by my surroundings.

> Whatever happens, conduct yourself in a manner worthy of the gospel of Christ. (Philippians 1:27a)

Rescue me through prayer:

Pray for my enemy and my situation. What did Jesus say about our enemy? "But I tell you, love your enemies and pray for those who persecute you, that you may be children of your Father in heaven" (Matthew 5:44–45a). If my enemy is a person, I have the opportunity to be obedient to God, pray for them, and share His love—again & again until God's will is done. My prayer should not be to take me away every time I don't like the situation I'm in.

Rescue me through relying on God's strength:

It is not by my strength that I can live surrounded by the enemy. "The Lord is my strength and my shield; my heart trusts in Him, and He helps me" (Psalm 28:7a). I am not in this battle alone. He walks by my side, and I draw upon His strength day by day.

Rescue me through claiming God's victory:

God has already won this battle, and I will know victory through Him.

> But thanks be to God! He gives us the victory through our Lord Jesus Christ. Therefore, my dear brothers and sisters, stand firm. Let nothing move you. Always give yourselves fully to the work of the Lord, because you know that your labor in the Lord is not in vain. (1 Corinthians 15: 57–58)

I can hide myself in the Lord. "For I hide myself in you" (Psalm 143:9b). I can draw so deep into His loving arms that the enemy only sees the Lord living through me. God is not going to let me hide in the basement. He wants me to hide in plain sight that all may know the work of God in my life.

How will others know? In the midst of the battles with my enemies, the fruit of the Spirit should be evident in my life.

> But the fruit of the Spirit is love, joy, peace, forbearance, kindness, goodness, faithfulness, gentleness and self-control. (Galatians 5:22–23a)

My Prayer

Lord, thank you that the battle is yours to fight and the victory is yours. No matter what my battle is, or will be, I can call on you. Teach me how to draw upon you in my responses and my attitude, so that others may see you at work in my life.

_____

_____

_____

_____

_____

_____

_____

_____

_____

_____

_____

_____

_____

_____

_____

_____

_____

_____

_____

_____

_____

_____

_____

God is My Go To

During my trip to Kaua'i, I noticed lots of wild chickens—everywhere. Pulling into a parking lot, a hen was just sitting there. She didn't move no matter how close the car came. After parking further away from her, she still sat there until all danger was gone. Then she got up and out came several baby chicks that were hiding under her wings—so adorable and so happy to be able to run around again. The chicks didn't wander far, and knew where to go to for safety.

> Hide me in the shadow of your wings. (Psalm 17:8b)

That was David's prayer to God when surrounded by his enemies in fear for his life. David knew his God would protect him.

From early childhood, David knew God. He knew how God would care for him. He knew God's love. He knew the power of his God. He knew that with one stone God would slay Goliath, the enemy of Israel.

As I read the Book of Psalms, I see David's relationship with God. In his victories and failures, in his strength and fears, and in his joy and sorrows, I see one trait. He goes to God for all things.

My life can be as David's life:

In my joy ....I go to God with a thankful heart. "My heart leaps for joy, and with my song I praise Him" (Psalm 28:7b).

In my sorrows ....I go to God for comfort. "May your unfailing love be my comfort" (Psalm 119:76a).

In my worries and need for direction...I go to God for wisdom. "I keep asking that the God of our Lord Jesus Christ, the glorious Father, may give you the Spirit of wisdom and revelation, so that you may know him better. I pray that the eyes of your heart may be enlightened in order that you may know the hope to which he has called you, the riches of his glorious inheritance in his holy people" (Ephesians 1:17–18).

In my loneliness ....I go to God to know His presence. "Blessed are those who have learned to acclaim you, who walk in the light of your presence, LORD" (Psalm 89:15).

In my victories ....I go to God and acknowledge by His hands I have had victory over my enemies. "How great is his joy in the victories you give!" (Psalm 21:1b).

In my day to day..............................I go to God for everything. "My soul thirsts for God, for the living God" (Psalm 42:2a).

God is right there for me, and always waiting for me to come. Under His wings I find all that I could ever need and so much more. "And my God will meet all your needs according to the riches of His glory in Christ Jesus" (Philippians 4:19).

My Prayer

Thank you, God that you are willing, ready, and always there to be my "go to". You are all I need. Forgive me when I think I can do it on my own. Open your wings—I'm coming in to stay for a while.

Homemaker

A Home with God

My mom was a traditional stay-at-home wife and mother—a homemaker. Being a homemaker wasn't about how clean the house was or making sure our laundry was done. Being a homemaker meant that she was there for my sister and me. Even after I grew up and out of the house, my parents' home was always open to us.

If I asked to come over for lunch, I'd walk into the smells of home cooking. One time it was homemade soup and cobbler. Who does that on short notice? I've been a career woman for many years, and you might get cold sandwiches at my house, but rarely anything from scratch at a moment's notice.

More than my mom's great cooking, coming to their house was like coming home. Their home was a take off your shoes, get comfortable, open the fridge, and help yourself type of home.

There was love in their home—a place to be loved and to give it in return. As my babies came along, they found the same love with them.

When our parents struggled with illness and grew more frail, my sister and I became the caretakers of our family—our parents and our own families.

After the loss of my parents and my divorce, I came to count on coming to my sister's home. Her home has always been the same as our parents' home—a home that was open, warm, inviting, and so full of love when I needed it the most.

In Psalm 5, David paints a beautiful picture of how much more our heavenly Father gives to us.

> In the morning, LORD, you hear my voice; in the morning I lay my requests before you and wait expectantly. (Psalm 5:3)

I know my God is there. I can take my prayers to Him every morning and wait—knowing I can put my trust in Him to take care of my needs. How precious a relationship with God I have found, to be able to wait expectantly.

> But I, by your great love, can come into your house, in reverence I bow down toward your holy temple. (Psalm 5:7)

Because God loves me so much, with a great love, His house is open to me. I can come in. What a comfort to know I'm always welcome. I always have a home.

> But let all who take refuge in you, be glad; let them ever sing for joy. Spread your protection over them, that those who love your name, may rejoice in you. (Psalm 5:11)

A home is not only full of love, but a place of joy. Knowing I can come in and find protection allows me to be free of the stress and worry in His presence. I am free to rejoice in this loving relationship.

My journey has brought me to a wonderful place that I can now open the door to my home. My home is open to not only my children, stepchildren, all their spouses and now grandbabies, but to so many more who call me mom, family and friend.

My Prayer

Thank you, God that I have been blessed to have had a loving home that gave me a glimpse into the wonderful home I have now with you. Teach me how to model this home, filled with your unconditional love, so others may know your love in my home.

The Treasures Within

> Blessed are all who take refuge in Him. (Psalm 2:12b)

To take refuge in God is to draw into His presence and to find shelter—away from the enemy, the harsh realities of the world, the struggles of the day, and the fears that bind. I can escape from what is outside, even if just for a moment. I can step away and come into God's presence to find shelter.

If I stand at the entrance of the shelter and keep looking outside, I will be safe and find rest. Yet, I will miss the treasures within. If I turn around and open my eyes and heart, I will find the treasures of living in His presence.

That's the "blessed" part of this verse. Sometimes I define blessed as fortunate or happy. The Hebrew definition is so much more—"God extends His benefits" or "enviable position from receiving God's provisions." Oh to be blessed as I take refuge in Him. Rather than staying on the edge of this relationship with God, I have the opportunity to turn around. I can come fully into His presence, and find the treasures within.

I have a picture of treasures in my mind: piles of treasures, chests of gold and jewels, or museums full of royal treasures. The picture fills me with awe and maybe even a little envy. Beautiful and enticing are the treasures of the world.

I would trade them all for the treasures I find in the presence of my God and His blessings in my life.

As I draw into His presence, I find a love that is not easily defined, because I can't live this love—this perfect love of God's. His love is the ultimate treasure.

What do I know about God's love?

I know I can never lose God's love. No matter what I do.

> For I am convinced that neither death nor life, neither angels nor demons, neither the present nor the future, nor any powers, neither height nor depth, nor anything else in all creation, will be able to separate us from the love of God that is in Christ Jesus our Lord. (Romans 8:38–39)

Each and every day His love is with me.

> May your unfailing love be with us, LORD, even as we put our hope in you. (Psalm 33:22)

God's love for me is so great that He gave His Son that I may have eternal life.

> For God so loved the world that He gave His one and only Son, that whoever believes in Him shall not perish but have eternal life. (John 3:16)

The depth of joy that I experience in my life is from the love and salvation that comes from God alone.

> But I trust in your unfailing love; my heart rejoices in your salvation. (Psalm 13:5)

Blessed am I, who takes refuge in Him. I am blessed by His love, a treasure to be found in His presence.

My Prayer

Draw me near to you, my Lord, that I may fully know your love. Help me to take my eyes off of the struggles outside of my shelter in you. Help me to focus instead on drawing nearer to you, and finding the treasures within.

After The Storm

*J*oy in Spring

Remember the Winter and Sing For Joy

From the first bud of the season to the hillside being in full bloom, spring is like the heavenly choir singing praises to our Lord.

> The mountains and hills will burst into song before you, and all trees of the fields will clap their hands. (Isaiah 55:12b)

What a wonderful time of the year is spring. I see new life after a very wet and harsh winter. The grounds are green with growth, plants are bigger than before, and flowers are vibrant with color. The view is so different from the browns of winter.

As with my life, God brings new life to a life that is lost and without purpose. The joy that fills my life is the joy that comes from my salvation—my decision to follow God.

> And there rejoice in your salvation. (Psalm 9:14b)

Do I live forever in spring after I come to know God? I wish I could say that could be true. My spiritual growth comes from experiencing the seasons. In the seasons, I can see God's work in my life, and know He is part of it all. I can then rejoice at what He has done in my life.

> For you make me glad by your deeds, LORD;
> I sing for joy at what your hands have done.
> (Psalm 92:4)

From the harsh sun in summer to freezing weather in winter, so I face the challenges of what lies ahead for me. Yet I have a place to take refuge.

> But let all who take refuge in you be glad; let them ever sing for joy. (Psalm 5:11a)

Yes, joy can be found in taking refuge under His wings, in His protection, and sheltered in His love. There I see God at work, and know His unfailing love for His children.

> You turned my wailing into dancing; you removed my sackcloth and clothed me in joy, that my heart may sing your praises and not be silent. LORD my God, I will praise you forever. (Psalm 30:11–12)

God turned my winter into spring. And when the seasons change once again, I can still rejoice. Why? Because I know my God is faithful. I have seen how He uses the winter and the storms, and makes something beautiful from them.

> The LORD has done great things for us, and we are filled with joy. (Psalm 126:3)

As I take in the beauty of the spring, I remember the winter. I remember that God's hands took the dead of winter to bring me spring. Praise Him! Sing for joy in spring.

My Prayer

Lord God, I thank you that you have a plan for my life. From the winter, you will create a beautiful spring in my life that is more beautiful than I can imagine. For by your grace I know I have a place with you. And I rejoice!

_____
_____
_____
_____
_____
_____
_____
_____
_____
_____
_____
_____
_____
_____
_____
_____
_____
_____
_____
_____
_____
_____
_____
_____
_____

When the Fog Lifts

A New Day

After a storm, the valley fills with fog—sometimes so thick you can't see anything in front of you. Where once I could see as far as the Sierras in the distance, I am not able to see even the road in the fog.

When I moved into my little town a few summers ago, I fell in love with my commute over the ridge to and from work. If I made it just right, I could see across the valley and watch the sun come up over the Sierras in the distance. "Good morning, God", I would say. I knew all was well.

One night late in the fall, after a storm, the fog settled in early. That once familiar road was now lost. I had to creep along the road, unsure of where the road would turn or dip. I thought I knew the road so well, but not that night.

In fact, I was shocked that the fog was there at all. I felt like someone should have told me about this, so I could have been prepared.

The storms of life are like that. I battle the storms through the help of God. "God is our refuge and strength, an ever present help in trouble" (Psalms 46:1). I come out on the other side victorious, but battle weary. Then the fog settles in—slowly at first until I am surrounded. I may not realize the fog is there, until I can't find my way.

For me, over the years, the fog has come in different ways. Sometimes the struggles at home or work have gone on for far too long, and I've just found myself to be battle weary. The fears of how I can make it through each day can overwhelm me. At times, depression took over.

Each time I found myself lost in the fog, not sure where to go. I needed to humble myself, and call upon the Lord. I needed to claim His place in my life.

> The Lord is great! (Psalm 70:4b)

> You are my help and my deliverer; LORD, do not delay. (Psalm 70:5b)

Each time, I found my way home through the fog. I made my way back home into God's loving arms, a shelter for healing and renewal.

> I sought the LORD, and He answered me; He delivered me from all my fears. (Psalm 34:4)

> For this God is our God forever and ever; He will be our guide ever to the end. (Psalm 48:14)

The fog may come, but I have a God who will guide me through every time.

I came over the ridge in the early morning, the Sierras in the distance, the valley full of trees below, covered in a light mist of morning fog. A beautiful reminder, I have a new day in God. The sun rising over the mountains singing praises to God. I sing along. Thanking God for bringing me out of the fog to a new day.

> Satisfy us in the morning with your unfailing love, that we may sing for joy and be glad all of our days. (Psalm 90:14)

My Prayer

Thank you, God that you are with me all through the storms, you guide me through the fog and shine upon me in the morning with your unfailing love.

_____

_____

_____

_____

_____

_____

_____

_____

_____

_____

_____

_____

_____

_____

_____

_____

_____

_____

_____

_____

_____

_____

_____

_____

_____

Songs of Deliverance

Looking Back with Joy

The tunnel is dark and quiet and I'm waiting for what will come next. I hear the clanking of the rails as we go ever higher and higher. I know the danger is coming. I'm barely breathing in anticipation. Why did I put myself here?! Then the danger is upon me, barreling at me, turn by turn. The pressure is pushing at me so hard I can barely breathe. I scream at the top of my lungs and then it's over. There's a pause and then the elated song of laughter is all around me. We all survived the ride.

The craziest thing happens next as I hear myself ask, "Can we go again?" What!!? Now that I know I'll survive, the thrill is exciting and safe. I find I want the joy and laughter that comes in the end.

Or I want to try a different ride. I want the excitement of going higher (but not too high), the thrill of the unknown, the turn me upside down moment, and the joy that the ride will end soon. I may even beg God to make this ride end. Those are the rides I never want to ever experience again.

Do you ever tell a story, months or years later, that was so scary at the time, but, now that it's all over, you laugh at it? My sister and I recall a time of being so afraid. There were noises outside, and we didn't know what they were. "Be quiet" she commanded. I could get on board with that. I'll be quiet and hide was my thought. But when something hit the outside of our room that was all it took. I was out of there looking for a safer place—right in the middle of my parents' bed. We can laugh about it now.

Life is full of ups and downs, scary places and situations, and long periods of darkness and unknown turns. We pray for the morning light or the ride to end. We look to God to save and protect us.

> You are my hiding place; you will protect me from trouble and surround me with songs of deliverance. (Psalm 32:7)

You are my hiding place: My favorite place to hide is with God. Shhh...don't tell anyone! It's a wonderful quiet place of prayer and a safe place to go. The key for me is to be quiet. I think of danger lurking outside, and I don't want to be found. I want only God and me to be together.

I can tell Him my fears, and listen to Him assure me of His love that will always be with me. I can hide in His strong loving arms, and find His quiet peace.

> For I have always been mindful of your unfailing love and have lived in reliance on your faithfulness. (Psalm 26:3)

You will protect me from trouble: I know where I will find safety. My God will see me through the storms, the turns, and the drops. He is my protector. As Jesus prayed to His Father, "protect them by the power of your name" (John 17:11b). There is no one greater than God.

And surround me with Songs of Deliverance: Just as I find laughter after the danger has passed or the thrill is over, so I can find joy and song in my heart that God has delivered me.

I sought the LORD, and He answered me; He delivered me from all my fears. (Psalm 34:4)

But I trust in your unfailing love; my heart rejoices in your salvation. I will sing the LORD's praise, for He has been good to me. (Psalm 13:5–6)

My Prayer

Lord God, you are my deliverer. I trust in you to see me through this crazy life and the adventures ahead. I am safe in your arms. Help me to see your faithfulness and rejoice in you. You are my song of deliverance.

_____

_____

_____

_____

_____

_____

_____

_____

_____

_____

_____

_____

_____

_____

_____

_____

_____

_____

_____

_____

_____

_____

_____

_____

Sing In The Morning

My Love Letter to God

I wonder what time it is. It's still dark outside. A definite sign I don't have to get up yet. I'll just lie here a little longer. Then I hear the birds celebrating a new day. A smile comes on my face. As the sun begins to rise higher, I see more light and the birds are becoming a hallelujah chorus. Oh, what joy the morning brings!

> But I will sing of your strength, in the morning I will sing of your love; for you are my fortress, my refuge in times of trouble. You are my strength, I sing praises to you; you, God, are my fortress, my God on whom I can rely. (Psalm 59:16–17)

I sing in the morning...don't you? It's a new day. The troubles of yesterday don't seem so big anymore. My body has had rest, and my strength has returned. I have let the worries go, and I have a fresh look on today. So I sing.

I sing because of His love...

> Satisfy us in the morning with your unfailing love, that we may sing for joy and be glad all our days. (Psalm 90:14)

There is nothing in this world that can satisfy me. I may try to find love, peace or joy out in the world. To be filled (satisfied) only comes from knowing the grace filled love of God. And because of that love, I can sing every day, every morning. The joy that fills my days comes only from that saving love of Jesus. So I sing.

I sing because of His strength...

He is my fortress, my refuge in times of trouble. If I look around, I see trouble. There's always something I can find— little troubles or big troubles. "Quit looking for them", I tell myself. I need to quit making a mountain out of a mole hill. God is my strength on which I can rely. If I put my trust in Him, I can sing in spite of the troubles that surround me. So I sing.

> God is our refuge and strength, an ever-present
> help in trouble. (Psalm 46:1)

I sing because my heart is full of praise to you God...

It's like the birds in the morning. I can't help it. I want to praise Him for who He is in my life, for all He has done for me, and for His amazing love. I don't just want to praise Him. I need to praise Him. It's my love letter back to Him. So I sing.

> I will praise the LORD all my life; I will sing
> praise to my God as long as I live. (Psalm 146:2)

The night has come again. Another busy day is behind me. I finally am ready to lay my burdens down and rest in Him. Tomorrow is a new day. Tomorrow brings a new morning, and I will sing of His love.

My Prayer

Oh, my Lord. I will sing to you a song of love. I will sing to you a song of praise. Each morning I yearn to start the day hearing your song of love to me. Teach me to listen for it. Teach me to sing in the morning.

My Everything

He is My Portion

On the screen I met my grandbabies for the first time—only 12 weeks old, approximately 2 inches long and still safe and secure in their mother's womb. Yes, I did say "babies", as in twins.

My daughter was everything these little ones needed for this part of their lives. She brought them the nutrients they needed. She was a safe place so they could grow each and every day. She kept them in a loving place where they knew nothing but her love. She was also their first lullaby, as she sang to them of God's love.

There's so much that she provided for them—a gentle touch, laughter, and her tender voice.

She was also their protector, a fierce protector. A mother who would do all she could to keep them safe for as long as she could.

Right now she is still everything they need.

How much more our loving God is everything we need. No matter what situation or place of need I find myself in, God is everything I need.

> I cry to you, LORD; I say, 'You are my refuge, my portion in the land of the living.' (Psalm 142:5)

David was desperate when he wrote of this time in his life. His back was up against the wall. He had no place to go but to turn to his God and to let God be his refuge—his safe place to come to.

And more than that, he knew God as his "portion". God was not just a piece of something bigger, but everything he needed.

Wow! I can't think of anything in my life that I can say that of, except God—not my career, not my husband, and not even my children. Not my money, my travels, and not my life experiences. None of these will ever be everything I need.

So why do I try to define what I need in earthly terms? "That was the perfect day, now I can face the world." "Now that I have this new job, I'll be able to settle down, buy a house, and start a family." "Even though I'm not feeling well, I'll just change my diet, exercise more, and get more rest, and then I'll be fine."

None of these are wrong thoughts, if I think I can handle things on my own. But you see I can't. Telling God my plans on how I'm going to "make things better" or "fix my life" is crazy! His plan is my journey. I can give each day and each situation my best and I know that whatever may come my way, I will give it to Him. As the saying goes, "Let go and let God".

What can the world give me compared to the riches I know I have in God? He is my portion, and the only one I need to turn to. Do I turn to Him only in times of trouble? No! I turn to Him in everything. He is my portion and everything I need.

Since He is my everything, I live a life in His love and in His hope. There is no place in my life for despair and worry.

> I say to myself, 'The LORD is my portion;
> therefore I will wait for Him.' (Lamentations 3:24)

What a wonderful place to be when I am in His presence. Knowing He is my portion, I will trust in Him. My days are filled with listening to His voice of love, growing closer to Him as we go through life together, and feeding on His Word. Just like my grandbabies depend on their mom to be their everything, I can depend on my God.

My Prayer

Lord, thank you that you are my everything. I can come to you each day, and you will be there. Teach me to come to you first and trust you with my life—all of it.

_____

_____

_____

_____

_____

_____

_____

_____

_____

_____

_____

_____

_____

_____

_____

_____

_____

_____

_____

_____

_____

_____

_____

_____

_____

_____

My Head Held High

Our body talks more than we are aware. Are you shy or confident? Happy or angry? Stressed or at peace? Some have learned to control what others see, while others are very open and show their feelings.

There are new studies about how to use your body stance to change how you are feeling. The concept of power stance, by Amy Cuddy, can be found in TED talks. She describes the impact of taking a Superman pose for 2 minutes before going into an interview or giving a speech, and how it changes hormone levels, thus your confidence.

As I prepare to step on the stage to speak, I go through a similar motion. Shoulders back, deep breath, head held high, and step out with confidence. One thing is different, I step out in confidence that God is with me.

> But you, LORD, are a shield around me, my glory,
> the One who lifts my head high. (Psalm 3:3)

As David is surrounded by his foes, he is confident in his God. He knows God. He knows that all will work out for God's glory, and he will be victorious in God.

What is my power stance? Where do I go to find confidence? Who is my strength?

First step of confidence comes from humbly bowing my head in prayer. "Humble yourselves before the Lord, and He will lift you up" (James 4:10). No matter my situation that I find myself in, I can let go of the fear and turn to God in prayer.

I will raise my hands in praise. I can't let the posture of fear keep me curled in a ball or my head down in weakness. Any stance of praise will take my focus off of me and my fears, and put my focus where it belongs, which is on God. I raise my hands in praise for His love, in praise for what He has done for me, and today in praise for who He is in the midst of what's going on. He is right there with me.

> I will praise you as long as I live, and in your name I will lift up my hands. (Psalm 63:4)

I need to take a moment and STOP! I sometimes (ok…many times) have to tell myself to stop running around like a crazy woman, as if everything has to be on my shoulders. The fear and chaos is mounting. Breathe! One of the best power stands for me is to stop, be still and acknowledge God.

> He says, 'Be still, and know that I am God.' (Psalm 46:10a)

He is my shield around me and He lifts my head high. I know that stance and walk oh so well. My shoulders back and head held high in confidence, not out of pride, but confidence in my God. He is my protector and my shield, and He walks with me. I am not alone. I am not defeated. I am His child.

My Prayer

Father God, as I look at my future and unknown outcomes, come along side me and let me know your presence. Help me to hear your call, and humble myself before you in prayer. I praise you in all my circumstances, because you know my journey and will be my guide. I look forward, in confidence and my head held high, to where you lead me.

_____

_____

_____

_____

_____

_____

_____

_____

_____

_____

_____

_____

_____

_____

_____

_____

_____

_____

_____

_____

_____

_____

_____

You Are My Lord, My God

Hope in Him

"I can't do it all!!" When my days are overwhelming, my body is exhausted, and my mind is full—in turmoil, scattered, and not able to focus—I just want to scream....STOP! I can't do it anymore! Where should I go? What should I do?

I should STOP, and look at my days, hours, and even minutes. What has my days been full of? "To Do" lists or God? Worries or God? Accomplishments or God?

So I need to stop to find a quiet place, and turn to God in prayer and be in His word.

I have a chair surrounded by bibles, journals, and daily devotionals. My personal place is set aside for one purpose, me and God. In my place, I pray...quiet my heart, O Lord, quiet my mind, give my body a moment of rest, let me draw near to you, and let you draw near to me.

There is rest and shelter in the shadow of His wings. I can hide there, even if just for a moment as the storm passes. He draws me into His loving arms (wings) that I may know His presence.

> Whoever dwells in the shelter of the Most High will rest in the shadow of the Almighty. (Psalm 91:1)

> He will cover you with His feathers, and under His wings you will find refuge; His faithfulness will be your shield and rampart. (Psalm 91:4)

Where is my hope? Is it in me or in God? I will fail and I hate that thought. Why do I need to be so perfect? I don't have to be when I'm in His presence. He accepts me just as I am. He will help me take my focus off me and what I can do, and I will put my hope in Him, His faithfulness and His unfailing love. He is always there for me without waiver. No matter what is going on around me, in me. Because of this…I can have hope.

> LORD, you alone are my portion and my cup; you make my lot secure. (Psalm 16:5)

> As for me, I will always have hope; I will praise you more and more. (Psalm 71:14)

Hope sets me free. I am free to let go of the worries and struggles. I am free of fear and the "what ifs" in my life. I am free of the burdens, and free to trust in a faithful God. Because I am free, I can SING. A heart that can sing is a heart that can say "thank you" in the midst of all that is going on, no matter what is happening. I can sing because my hope is in the Lord, my God. My hope is not in me.

> Because you are my help, I sing in the shadow of your wings. (Psalm 63:7)

God…You are my portion….everything I need

You are my strength…in my weakness

You are my refuge…when I'm afraid

You are my joy…when my heart is burdened

You are my everything…my Lord, my God

My Prayer

As for me, Lord, I'm your child. I want my life to reflect you as I go through the tough times. I do not ask those times to be removed, or ask for the easy way out. The journey is mine to take, but not mine alone. I go through this journey, each and every day, with you God. May I glorify you in all I do.

God, My Deliverer

God Glorified in My Life

> LORD my God, I take refuge in you; save and
> deliver me from all who pursue me. Psalm 7:1

Another night of tossing and turning. I'm really good at wrestling with my thoughts throughout the night. I know that the wrestling will not solve anything—be it worry for family, deadlines at work, unhealthy relationships, fear of what I have to face tomorrow, or just reliving the past. These thoughts can crowd out the peace that comes from God. When I am wrestling with my thoughts, my mind is not in alignment with God.

The psalmist describes it so well in Psalm 77. "When I was in distress, I sought the Lord" (Psalm 77:2a). That's where I start… then it turns to wrestling. "At night I stretched out untiring hands, and I would not be comforted" (v. 2b). "I thought about the former days, the years of long ago" (v. 5). Then I doubt, "will the Lord reject me forever?" (v7a). And so goes the night and even the following day.

Where am I putting my trust? I know I need to align myself with God. I pray *"Lord, my God"*, a reminder that He is the Lord, my God. He is the one who loves me, cares for me, and the One God. When I acknowledge that I can take refuge in Him, I can come into His presence, seek Him, and find that I can put my trust in Him.

The psalmist in Psalm 77 continues. "Then I thought" (v. 10a). That's the sweet moment when I realize that I have been worrying and wrestling with my enemies on my own. I should be remembering how many times God has been there to deliver me from mine enemies and seen me through the challenges of life. "I will remember the deeds of the LORD; yes, I will remember your miracles of long ago" (v. 11). I will remember not just God's work in my life, but other lives, and even remembering His works from the beginning of time. "Your ways, God, are holy. What god is as great as our God?" (v. 13).

"Your path led through the sea, your way through the mighty waters, though your footprints were not seen" (v. 19). The psalmist is recalling God's mighty deeds in delivering the Israelites from the pursuit of their enemy, the Egyptians. Even though God had freed them from Pharaoh and brought them out of Egypt, their doubt and fear came back once again.

"Moses answered the people, 'Do not be afraid. Stand firm and you will see the deliverance the LORD will bring you today. The Egyptians you see today you will never see again. The LORD will fight for you; you need only to be still' " (Exodus 14:13–14). I don't have to fight my battles alone. I just need to be still and trust in God.

Why is it so important that I let God "save and deliver me from those who pursue me" (Psalm 7:1b)? So that God may be glorified in my life. Others will see it is God who is in the fight. "And the Egyptians said, 'Let's get away from the Israelites! The LORD is fighting for them against Egypt' " (Exodus 14:25b).

Not only does the enemy see God at work, but so do the children of God. "And when the Israelites saw the mighty hand of the LORD displayed against the Egyptians, the people feared the LORD and put their trust in him and in Moses his servant" (Exodus 14:31).

All through the Old Testament, the enemy (entire nations) had heard of "Israel's God" and would not do battle.

It is God at work in my life. I can stop wrestling with my enemies who pursue me, and put my trust in "the Lord, my God". I can find refuge, a safe place, in His presence.

My Prayer

Lord, bring to mind the many times you have been in front of me in the battles and have delivered me. This is not my battle so that I get the glory. May the glory be yours and yours alone.

Earthquake Resistant

I Will Not Be Shaken

Asleep in bed, I'm awakened in the middle of the night. The bed was being shaken. It felt like a giant picked up the home, shook it and dropped it back down. Earthquake! The worst one I'd ever been in, but mild in perspective. Only an after-shock, we were told. My heart raced with fear to get to my baby who was in another room, only to find out later she slept through it all.

I've lived in California my whole life and have only experienced a few mild earthquakes. I've seen so much damage occur to buildings, even during small ones. I hear of buildings being retrofitted to become earthquake safe, in hope of minimizing the damage.

Sometimes earthquakes come in the form of a life event—something unexpected and life changing. Your life is shaken hard. Your normal routine is no longer possible. Your physical or mental abilities are diminished. Your loved one is no longer by your side. Many life events will come. You can count on them. Just like those of us in California know, that at some point in our life, an earthquake will come.

> Truly He is my rock and my salvation; He is my fortress, I will not be shaken. (Psalm 62:6)

Engineers know that if a building's foundation is on soft ground, the whole building may crumble to the ground during an earthquake. In the "earthquakes" of my life, I have definitely been shaken but not destroyed. Why? I have built my life on a firm foundation. My Rock is Jesus.

As a young girl, I didn't know what life was all about. I felt like something was missing. That was because no one had told me about Jesus yet. He was the missing piece I needed.

David says it well. "Truly He…is my salvation." My parents, my church, my culture have nothing to do with my salvation and my decision to follow Christ. This is a very personal decision. Do I or do I not want to give my life to Jesus. I said I do. Step One to building my house upon my Rock.

> If you declare with your mouth, 'Jesus is Lord,'
> and believe in your heart that God raised Him
> from the dead, you will be saved. (Romans 10:9)

Every foundation begins with placing the cornerstone. Jesus is my precious cornerstone. As a believer, Jesus becomes the center of my life and my life is built upon Him…Step Two.

> Consequently, you are no longer foreigners or strangers, but fellow citizens with God's people and also members of His household, built on the foundation of the apostles and prophets, with Christ Jesus himself as the chief cornerstone. In Him the whole building is joined together and rises to become a holy temple in the Lord. And in Him you too are being built together to become a dwelling in which God lives by His Spirit. (Ephesians 2:19–22)

How I'm building on top of my foundation in Christ is critical to the stability of my life. Will I roll with the earthquakes or crumble? I've seen pictures of buildings being completely knocked from their foundations. Engineers know that one solution is to tie the foundation to the building, so the whole structure moves as a unit.

That's a perfect example of what I need to do—tie myself closely to Jesus so my building and foundation move as one...Step Three. I can build on my own, but without Christ in the center of my life, connected to all my decisions and life choices, my building stands alone and will fall. My building (my life) built on God's Word is connected to Jesus. We are tied together, and will not "be shaken" when the earthquakes come.

> Nevertheless, God's solid foundation stands firm, sealed with this inscription: 'The Lord knows those who are His,' and, "Everyone who confesses the name of the Lord must turn away from wickedness.' (2 Timothy 2:19)

I am His and together we build this house to stand firm on the solid foundation. In God, I will find refuge and not be shaken.

My Prayer

Lord, help me to build this house on the strong foundation I have in you. Show me when I am building on my own, building with substandard materials or letting rot come into my house. I draw near to you so we move as one.

As Long As I live

A Love Better Than Life

"Till death do us part' is a familiar wedding vow for a bride and groom—a vow that they will cherish and love each other forever.

There is something wonderful in witnessing true love. I'm a big fan of romance movies, romantic comedies, and romance novels. They give us the first glance, first kiss, vows of forever love, and then a parting view of an elderly couple walking down the road still holding hands and still in love. You just know their words of love are for "as long as I live". Ahhh…true love.

I don't want to just witness this "perfect" love. I want to experience a love that is overwhelming, beautiful, pure, and never ending. And I have that love from God. His love fills me and makes me whole. I am loved.

Psalm 63 is a beautiful love song David wrote to God, and I have experienced this love song in the love relationship I have with my God.

A love that seeks and thirsts for you, God.

> You, God, are my God, earnestly I seek you; I thirst for you; my whole being longs for you. (v. 1a)

A love that knows God's glory and sees His beauty.

> I have seen you in the sanctuary and beheld your power and your glory. (v. 2)

A love that has no boundaries on His love.

> Because your love is better than life. (v. 3a)

A love that wants to tell the world of His love.

> My lips will glorify you. I will praise you as
> long as I live, and in your name I will lift up my
> hands. (v. 3b–4)

I can draw into this love, and let Him take me in His arms and
be loved. My heart will sing as I release my burdens, and let
myself be loved by God.

> Because you are my help, I sing in the shadow of
> your wings. (v. 7)

As long as I live, God's love for me will never end. The more
I draw near to Him in every part of my life I experience His
love--a perfect love.

My Prayer

God, I am humbled that you would love me, in spite of all my flaws. You see me through the eyes of Jesus, and love me. I sing to the mountain tops of your love and I quietly enjoy sitting in your presence filled with your love. As long as I live, I will love you and long for you. Wrap me in the shadow of your wings, and hear my heart sing of my love for you.

_____
_____
_____
_____
_____
_____
_____
_____
_____
_____
_____
_____
_____
_____
_____
_____
_____
_____
_____
_____
_____
_____
_____